A Vet on the Farm

by Karra McFarlane

illustrated by Tom Jellett

OXFORD
UNIVERSITY PRESS
AUSTRALIA & NEW ZEALAND

Asha is a vet.

She visits farms.

Farmer Nick has a sheep dog.

Asha meets Rex with her vet gear.

Rex will feel well now.

Liz has a cow.

Meg has hurt her rear leg.

Asha sits on a chair to look at Meg.

She fixes the rear leg.

She checks it is secure.

Meg feels good now.

Asha hops back to avoid the manure!

Jon has a goat.

Dot has a pain in her ear.

Asha checks her ear.

She puts powder in the ear.

The bell rings.

It is Nick, Liz and Jon. They are all waiting for Asha.